THE GAME OF LOVE AND CHANCE

MARIVAUX

THE GAME OF
LOVE AND CHANCE

translated and adapted by Neil Bartlett

OBERON BOOKS
LONDON

WWW.OBERONBOOKS.COM

First published in 1992 by Oberon Books Ltd
521 Caledonian Road, London N7 9RH
Tel: +44 (0) 20 7607 3637 / Fax: +44 (0) 20 7607 3629
e-mail: info@oberonbooks.com
www.oberonbooks.com

A catalogue record for this book is available from the British Library.

PB ISBN: 978-0-94823-058-5

Cover design by James Illman

Visit www.oberonbooks.com to read more about all our books
and to buy them. You will also find features, author interviews and
news of any author events, and you can sign up for e-newsletters
so that you're always first to hear about our new releases.

Introduction

What follows is the script as it stood at the end of the second week of rehearsal. When originally delivered to the company, it came with the following explanatory notes.

The Time

The play – the game of the title – takes place in two historical periods simultaneously: then and now. (This is of course true of any new production of an old play). The 'then' of our production is sometime in the middle 1930s; the 'now' is the night of the actual performance. The language of the script is rooted in a theatricalised memory of the 1930s – but the performers, since they are contemporary actors, not just 'real' 1930s people, are also allowed and obliged to quote other theatrical styles – they sometimes seem to be grabbing quotations off the dressing room rail of theatre history and using them as they see fit. At times this may create the effect that they are improvising, not acting.

The Place

Onstage is a 1930s interior representing the reception room of an upper-class family house – panelled walls, a telephone, an ashtray, a grand piano: the bare necessities of civilised life. There are five doors: one leading to the main staircase of the house; one leading to the guest rooms; and three discreetly concealed staff doors. This onstage area is governed by the strict rules of pre-war etiquette. Offstage there is all the usual paraphernalia – props tables, mirrors, worn out armchairs, old copies of newspapers, packets of Silk Cut, dirty coffee mugs. (Again, this is the set-up for most productions of old plays. The only difference here is that in our production both areas are visible to the audience.)

The Script

My suggestions of possible non-verbal actions are exactly that: suggestions. It does seem to me crucial that we see some of the encounters that the text itself does not describe.

The punctuation of Marivaux is very difficult to understand on the page. Sometimes it is used to give a very specific shape to lines, and sometimes it is much more shapeless – the characters just talk and talk with endless semi-colons to indicate pauses for breath. The punctuation of the translation should therefore be taken with great care: sometimes it is there for precise effect; sometimes I have used dashes or semi-colons to indicate pauses that may end up being commas, dashes or even full stops depending on the performer's taste and instincts. All opportunities allowed by the period language for eccentricities of stress should be extravagantly exploited.

Nationality

Arlecchino is Italian, and English is his second language. Lisette is English (we may be sure that her real name isn't Lisette: she only uses that name in her professional capacity as coiffeuse). Marivaux's Mario has become Maurice, because I didn't want anyone to wonder why he wasn't Italian. Monsieur Orgon has become Mr Prowde and Dorante has become Mr Dorant. Silvia is Silvia.

Repetitions

You will see that I have proposed several places where text is repeated. This is my own invention, but is inspired by the original. Characters are always reusing words and lines from earlier scenes in their dialogues; they themselves often attempt to go back to the beginnings of scenes and start again, and in the extraordinary speech which Silvia makes describing Dorante's exit in the third act Marivaux himself seems to propose a speech which is that of an actor meditating on and replaying a theatrical moment, rather than that of an actor pretending to talk like a real person in real life. Some of the repetitions reflect my own experience of translating the play, in that they offer different readings of the same line. All of these repetitions are optional.

The original production was cast before this translation was made, and each part was written for a particular performer. This influenced the production in three crucial ways. Firstly, any production of the play must recognise that the role of Arlecchino can properly only be played by a real Harlequin, not an actor. Anyone who wants to do it must find their own distinctive solution to this problem. The Arlecchino in the first production was Marcello Magni, who played Marivaux's text in several languages simultaneously; Italian, English, French, Mime and Slapstick were prominent. Where his lines are printed [in square brackets] this indicates that I have provided a literal translation of the French which must then be used by the performer concerned as the basis for his performance. Secondly, the role of Maurice was treated very distinctively (high-handedly), because it was written to be played by a singer-pianist. He played most of his scenes (and several others) seated at the grand piano, which was in the centre of the set, providing appropriate (or devastatingly inappropriate) accompaniment to the action – in the form of either set-piece songs, or the apparently random but in fact very pointed tinklings of a dressing-gowned, chain-smoking 1930s queen. Thirdly, our Silvia was considerably older than our Dorant. We weren't interested in making a show about the confusions of an *ingénue* – we wanted to make a show about just how much someone who has very good reasons to be single has to lose when they fall in love with someone in every way unsuitable.

This script contains echoes of other scripts and I would like you to be aware of these as you are reading. Coward (*The Vortex* and *Brief Encounter*), Congreve (*Love for Love*) and old scripts for *Upstairs Downstairs* were much in my mind as I wrote.

This translation would not have been possible if Mr James Gardiner had not made me understand what Silvia means when she says, 'Ah, now I see how my heart works'. My thanks to him for that, and for listening patiently to all of the first four versions of the script in their entirety.

Neil Bartlett

Characters

MR PROWDE
The Father. A Widower

SILVIA
The Daughter. A Society Woman

MAURICE
The Brother. A Bachelor

LISETTE
The Maid. A distant relative of that 'thoroughly
experienced French maid' referred to by Lady
Bracknell in *The Importance of Being Earnest*

MR DORANT
The Suitor. An Eligible Young Man,
recently down from College

ARLECCHINO
The Chauffeur. An Italian

The Suitor's name is pronounced 'Durrant'.

This translation of *The Game of Love and Chance* was first performed in October 1992. The production was commissioned and co-produced by Gloria and the Cambridge Theatre Company in association with the Royal National Theatre. The cast was as follows:

SILVIA, Maggie Steed

LISETTE, Caroline Quentin

MR PROWDE, Trevor Baxter

MAURICE, Stefan Bednarczyk

MR DORANT, Peter Wingfield

ARLECCHINO, Marcello Magni

Directors Mike Alfreds and Neil Bartlett

Designer Paul Dart

Movement Leah Hausman

Music Nicolas Bloomfield

A piano is being played.
We see four men – THE FATHER, THE BROTHER, THE SUITOR and
THE CHAUFFEUR. Seen as a quartet, they seem ominous, even sinister.
They seem very definitely a quartet, a team, a foursome.
We also see THE MAID, going about her business, and clearly not having
anything to do with them. If there are sides in this game then she is
definitely not on theirs.
We then see SILVIA, absolutely on her own. She has her back to us; when
she turns we see that she is perfectly dressed and perfectly made up. One
gets the impression that she has already had several cups of coffee. Either
she is dying for a cigarette or she is smoking one. Not only does she have
to deal with what her maid has just told her, she has to deal with an
audience as well.
SILVIA makes her own rather free but nonetheless accurate translation of
Monsieur Marivaux's opening line. She says: WHAT THE HELL HAS IT
GOT TO DO WITH YOU? and then, immediately, the play begins.

Act One

SCENE 1

(*Morning.*
We jump-cut straight into the middle of a conversation. Throughout
this conversation, LISETTE is at work with coffee cups, dressing gowns,
clothes, ashtrays et cetera, the morning routine, continually exiting and
entering.)

SILVIA: Alright, I'll say it again; you had no right to interfere.
Since when did *you* answer for *my* feelings?

LISETTE: I did think that on this one particular occasion your
feelings might resemble those of every other woman in
the world. The Master your father asked me if you were
reconciled to the idea of his wanting to get you married,
if you relished the prospect; and so I said yes I said. Well
obviously I did. And quite possibly you're the only single
woman in the entire world in regard to whom The Yes
wouldn't be the right answer. The No isn't natural.

SILVIA: 'The No isn't natural.' What a ridiculous line. I take it
that you find the prospect of marriage utterly charming.

LISETTE: Definitely The Yes once again.

SILVIA: That'll do. Go and exercise your impertinence elsewhere – and in future, it is not your place to judge my heart according to the workings of yours.

LISETTE: My heart's made just like everybody else's. I don't see why yours has taken it into its head to be made like nobody's.

SILVIA: Honestly, if she had the nerve, she'd come right out with it and call me a...an eccentric.

LISETTE: If she had your money we'd soon see.

SILVIA: Lisette, you are trying to be trying.

LISETTE: I was hardly trying at all. I don't see what great harm there was in me telling him you don't mind the idea of getting married.

SILVIA: Firstly...you didn't quite tell the truth. I am *not* bored with being single.

LISETTE: News to me.

SILVIA: It is, secondly, not appropriate that my father should think his idea of marrying me off gives me any great pleasure, since that may lead him to pursue it with a confidence that may well prove groundless.

LISETTE: What? You're not going to marry the one he's picked you?

SILVIA: How should I know? Perhaps he won't be to my taste – that's why I'm so tense.

LISETTE: I heard he's a real gentleman – well spoken, well dressed. Well built. I heard you couldn't possibly get one who had a better temper or a better sense of humour; what more d'you want, sounds to me like the ideal husband.

SILVIA: 'The Ideal Husband'. Where do you acquire these expressions?

LISETTE: Lord knows, madam, it's rare enough for a gentleman of his quality to want to do things properly these days; if he came round courting most women of my acquaintance would have him without standing on any sort of ceremony. Well put together, that's what you need in private; well mannered and well spoken, that's what you need when you're out in Society. Practical and decorative: he's got the lot.

SILVIA: Yes he has, pictured like that, and one hears it's quite a good likeness, but one only hears, and when one sees one mayn't concur in the general verdict. Apparently he is singularly good looking, which I find rather unattractive in a man.

LISETTE: Well that's a very modern idea.

SILVIA: It's a very sensible idea. How often one has remarked on the vanity of the handsome.

LISETTE: Oh he's wrong being vain but he's alright being handsome.

SILVIA: And they do say he's got a terrific physique. Oh well –

LISETTE: Oh well yes I'm sure we could forgive him that.

SILVIA: Handsome, distinguished – I find it all so very superficial.

LISETTE: Yes madam, well if I ever get married, I assure you I shall find it all very necessary.

SILVIA: You don't know what you're talking about. In marriage, one requires the reasonable, not the desirable. Actually, all I'm looking for is decency, and that's harder to find in a man than people think. This one comes highly recommended; but I don't know anyone who's actually sampled the goods. Men are so prone to making false claims about themselves. Especially the clever ones. And I should know, knowing as I do the most eligible men in town. It's all so charming, so very reasonable, so very amusing, they all look as smart as indeed one finds they are. 'He looks a decent sort, such a dependable, solid sort', one used to hear that all the time about Tom. 'Well he is,' people used to say. I myself used to say: 'What you see is what you get with Tom.' Oh yes, there's a face one can trust, so charming, so considerate, so easily transformed a quarter of an hour later into that of an aggressive boor who terrorises an entire household. Tom got married: and now that's all his wife, his children and his staff ever see of him, while he still goes about town parading the friendly physiognomy by which we all recognise him and which is in fact nothing but a mask he puts on with his hat whenever he leaves the house.

LISETTE: How peculiar to have two faces.

SILVIA: And doesn't everyone take one look at Dick and instinctively adore him? Well, in the privacy of his own home the man never utters a word, never laughs, never even lets slip a sigh; he's not so much incommunicative as inert: ice, inside. His own wife has no idea what's going on in his head; they never talk; she's married to a kind of frigid recluse who only ever leaves his study to come down to dinner – at which he then makes the whole table simply die of depression, chilliness and boredom. What fun that must be.

LISETTE: I'm catching a cold hearing you describe him. And what about that Harry?

SILVIA: What about that Harry? The other day they had had some sort of a row; I called; I was announced, and I watched him come down to greet me with open arms, charm itself; from the way he was smiling one would have thought I had merely interrupted some quite inconsequential conversation. The beast. That's what men are like. One would never have known that his wife was in tears. Over him. I found her in a complete state, white as a sheet, eyes ruined with all that weeping. I found her in the sort of state in which I may one day find myself. I recognised my future self in that portrait, my probable destiny as a cheap reproduction. I felt sorry for her, Lisette: imagine, one day, you may feel sorry for me. What an appalling idea. So there you have him. 'The Husband.' What do you think?

LISETTE: 'The Husband.' Is a husband. It was a mistake to end up with that word because it's made me forget all the rest. (*Enter MR PROWDE.*)

SCENE 2

PROWDE: Good morning, daughter. I trust you'll find the news to your liking…your young man arrives this morning; his father has just informed me of as much in this letter. 'But answer came there none.' … You look unhappy. And Lisette looks at the floor. Now what's all that about? You tell me then Lisette; what is the matter?

LISETTE: Oh sir, one face that gives you the shakes, another that makes you catch your death; one set of insides (frozen) that keep themselves very much to themselves, oh and of course the depressed portrait with the white sheet and the red eyes; that, sir, is the matter we have been working so hard at getting ourselves into a state over.

PROWDE: What is she talking about? Insides, portraits, someone'll have to explain, it's all beyond me.

SILVIA: I've been entertaining Lisette with 'The Misfortunes of The Unhappily Married Woman' – I cited the case of Harry's wife, who I found the other day horribly depressed because her husband had just shouted at her; I was simply making a few observations on that topic.

LISETTE: Ah yes, friendly physiognomies; we were observing that The Husband wears a mask for work and a frown for the wife.

PROWDE: From which, I take it, I am to understand that the prospect of marriage, daughter, alarms you – and all the more so because you have not met the young man in question.

LISETTE: Firstly, he's good looking, which is a real shame.

PROWDE: A shame? Lisette, are you feeling quite well this morning? A shame?

LISETTE: I only speak as I'm spoken at; that's Madam's theory and I'm sticking to it.

PROWDE: Yes well never mind all that now. My dear, you know how much I love you. Mr Dorant is coming here to court you – now I made this arrangement when I was last down in the country, where his father is my oldest and my dearest friend – but it was made on the condition that the pair of you get on; I forbid you to make any allowance for my feelings in this matter. If he isn't to your liking, then you just say the word, he'll be sent packing; and if you shouldn't be to his – well back he goes just the same.

LISETTE: Shouldn't take more than one number then:
(*LISETTE sings snatches of two popular songs of the period, one illustrating MR PROWDE's first scenario – that the pair will be well matched and will get married – and the second illustrating*

his second – that they'll be ill matched and will swiftly part.
Her contribution to the debate is ignored.)

PROWDE: I myself have never actually met this Dorant, he was
away when I was down at his father's place, but to judge by
what I'm told about him I confidently predict that neither
of you will want to send the other packing.

SILVIA: I'm touched by how sweet you're being about all of
this, Daddy. You've forbidden me to make any allowances
and I shall do exactly as you say.

PROWDE: As I insist.

SILVIA: But I was wondering, and I feel embarrassed asking
really, because I've only just thought of it, if you might
grant me one small favour; it would make me feel so much
more relaxed about the whole thing.

PROWDE: You can but ask; if it's that small, I'll grant it.

SILVIA: Oh it's minute, but I'm afraid you'll think I'm taking
advantage of how good to me you are.

PROWDE: Take it, dear girl; you know these days one has to be
a little too good to be true in order to be truly good.

LISETTE: Only a really nice man could get away with a line
like that.

PROWDE: Tell me what it is I can do for you, my daughter.

SILVIA: He's due here this morning, if only I could see him,
study him a little without him knowing it was me. Lisette is
good at charades, she could take my place for a little while,
and I could take hers.

PROWDE: What a charming idea... Allow me a moment's
consideration of your proposal. If I let her do it, the
charade may turn out to be a little more original than
she expects... Very well, my dear, I shall allow you your
change of role. Do you think you will be able to manage
yours, Lisette?

LISETTE: Me, sir, oh you know what I'm like. 'Try any chat
on with me and see where it gets you, sunshine. This
physiognomy 'ere merely 'ints at my 'igh Society ways and
means of dealing with the likes of you.' Well? What d'you
think? Recognise Lisette then do you?

PROWDE: Quite remarkable. Even I was completely taken in.
But good heavens, is that the time! – off, off and get ready

– we don't want Mr Dorant catching us unawares – haste, haste – and make sure the rest of the staff are told.

SILVIA: I really shan't need more than an apron.

(*LISETTE, who was already on her way to get to those frocks, stops in her tracks. She takes off her apron, and drops it for SILVIA to pick up. When she speaks, she does not crudely parody a caricatured Society Lady; she now mimics SILVIA, in particular and with complete accuracy.*)

LISETTE: And I really must go and see to my face; Lisette, you may as well begin to acquaint yourself with your duties by doing my hair…a little promptitude while we're working, if you don't mind.

SILVIA: (*Fighting back with an imitation of equal accuracy.*) Oh madam, I'm sure I'll soon have you sorted out. Alright? (*Exit LISETTE. Enter MAURICE.*)

SCENE 3

MAURICE: Sister dear, congratulations, I've just heard. So, we're going to *meet* this young man of yours.

SILVIA: Brother dear, yes. But I've got things to be getting on with so you will have to ask Father for all the details, do excuse me.

(*Exit SILVIA.*)

SCENE 4

PROWDE: Let her go, Maurice, I can tell you all you need to know.

MAURICE: I take it there's news, pater.

PROWDE: I would just say, by way of a preface, that I am only telling you this on the understanding that I do so in complete confidence.

MAURICE: Absolutely.

PROWDE: We *are* going to meet Mr Dorant today; but we are going to meet him in disguise.

MAURICE: In disguise. Is he coming in fancy dress – oh God, you're going to give him a party.

PROWDE: …here's the relevant paragraph in the father's letter… 'Moreover I have no idea what your reaction will

be to a scheme which my son has lately dreamt up – it is a
little hare-brained, as even he admits – but seems to spring
from honourable and even sensible motives – namely,
he has requested my permission to arrive at your house
disguised as his own chauffeur – who will in turn be
impersonating his master.'

MAURICE: Now that will be amusing.

PROWDE: Listen to the rest – 'My son remains entirely serious
about his pending engagement. He hopes, he says, while
temporarily so disguised, to observe the character of his
intended and to get to know her a little so that he may
properly make up his mind with regard to his future – we
did after all agree that he should be free to make it up for
himself. Personally I trust entirely your glowing accounts
of your daughter and so have consented to the whole thing
while taking the precaution of alerting you – despite a
request from him that I should keep you in the dark. It's up
to you whether or not you tell the lucky girl herself.' And
there is now an additional complication. Your sister, herself
a little anxious on the subject of this Dorant – and as yet
unaware of his little scheme – has requested my permission
to stage her own version of the very same charade in order
to observe him precisely as he wishes to observe her. Well?
A rather…original situation, don't you think? Maid and
Mistress are at this very minute on-ing with the motley.
What would you advise, Maurice? Do I tell your sister or
not?

MAURICE: Frankly, Father, if that's the lie of the land I think
I should respect the happy coincidence of their having
had the same idea at the same time; and indeed ensure they
are provided with every opportunity to practise their mutual
deception. Let's see if their hearts find each other out. Perhaps
Mr Dorant will take a fancy to my sister *en soubrette* which
would be charming for her.

PROWDE: Let's see her get out of this one.

MAURICE: It can hardly fail to be diverting. Personally I shall
be booking a seat in the front row and offering our happy
couple every possible encouragement.

SCENE 5

(*MAURICE rings the bell. Enter SILVIA.*)

SILVIA: You rang, m'sieur? How do I do as The Maid. You apparently know what's occurring, brother dear; what's your verdict?

MAURICE: I should say, sister dear, that the chauffeur doesn't have a hope in hell – and I shouldn't be at all surprised if The Maid steals The Master from under her Mistress's nose.

SILVIA: Actually I don't think I should at all mind him falling for me while I'm in character. I should quite enjoy driving him a little mad, dizzying him a little as he teeters on the edge of the social chasm yawning between us. If this can do that for me then I shall be happy – and indeed proud – to wear it. Besides it'll help me to find out what he's really like. As for his chauffeur, I hardly think I need fear any advances from that quarter; I'm sure even in this my innate refinement of feature will inspire respect rather than any nonsense from the likes of him.

MAURICE: Careful; you are now the likes of him.

PROWDE: And he is bound to find you attractive.

SILVIA: Well I'm sure I can turn that honour to my advantage; chauffeurs always love to talk; lovers talk too much, and so I shall make him tell me *all* about his master.

(*Either the phone rings, or the Stage Manager comes on – either way, LISETTE can't deliver it because she's too busy dressing up – but MR PROWDE gets the message that DORANT has arrived in disguise as his own servant.*)

PROWDE: Well send him up. Dorant's chauffeur is here. His master seems to have been delayed slightly on some business matter. Where's Lisette?

SILVIA: Lisette is dressing, and is advised by her mirror that we are most unwise to deliver Mr Dorant up to her tender mercies; she's nearly ready.

(*There is a knock at the door.*)

PROWDE: Steady on – here we go.

SCENE 6

(*They arrange themselves. Enter DORANT, carrying luggage.*)

DORANT: I'm looking for a Mr Prowde; is it to him that I have the honour of offering my services?

PROWDE: Indeed, my boy, it is.

DORANT: Sir, as I hope you have been informed, I am here on behalf of Mr Dorant, who will be following shortly, and who has sent me on ahead to assure you of his best respects until such time as he can do so in person.

PROWDE: You have taken his place most graciously. Lisette, what do you think of this lad here?

SILVIA: Me, sir, I think he is quite welcome. And quite promising.

DORANT: You are too kind. I do the best I can.

MAURICE: And quite striking, really. Let's hope your affections aren't tempted to stray from the straight and narrow, Lisette.

SILVIA: My affections, oh sir, that's quite another matter.

DORANT: Don't mind him, young lady, Sir fancies me more than I do myself.

SILVIA: How much I admire modesty in a man. Pray continue in that vein.

MAURICE: Oh, very good, one might almost think the title of 'Young Lady' were appropriate. Listen, if you people are going to be so formal with the introductions you'll be standing on ceremony all day. Let's be a bit more familiar shall we? She's Lisette, and you, dear boy, what d'you call yourself?

DORANT: Birmingham, sir, at your service.

SILVIA: Alright. 'Hello Birmingham.'

DORANT: Oh really? 'Hello Lisette.' At your service.

MAURICE: 'At your service', no, no, not at all the correct usage – try 'I'm all yours'.

(*MR PROWDE laughs.*)

SILVIA: (*To MAURICE.*) You're making a fool of me.

DORANT: If there's any call for familiarity I leave that up to Lisette here.

SILVIA: You feel free, Birmingham, go on and break the bleedin' ice if that makes the Master 'ere 'appy.

DORANT: Ta very much, Lisette, and I'm only too glad to respond to your civility in kind.

PROWDE: Never mind, my dears; perhaps you'll find yourselves falling in love, then all these social niceties will seem somehow…irrelevant.

MAURICE: Steady on; falling in love, that's quite another matter – or perhaps you are unaware of my own, personal, interest in Lisette's heart. True – it spurns me as yet – but I don't want Birmingham trespassing on my property.

SILVIA: Oh, really! Is that how you want to play it? Well I wish Birmingham would fall in love with me.

DORANT: There was really no need to have said that, Lisette; your wish is my command without you having to say a word.

MAURICE: Mister Birmingham, you must have picked that little compliment up somewhere very special.

DORANT: Indeed I did sir, I found it lying in her eyes.

MAURICE: That will do thank you; I can't abide smart remarks from the staff.

SILVIA: He's not making them at your expense; and if I've got something in my eye, then he's welcome to it.

PROWDE: I think you're losing the argument, my boy, let's go. Mr Dorant will be here at any moment, and we should inform my daughter – and you, Lisette, show this lad which is his master's room. Goodbye, Birmingham.

(*MR PROWDE shakes DORANT's hand.*)

DORANT: Sir, you're too kind.

(*Exit MR PROWDE and MAURICE.*)

SCENE 7

SILVIA: I'm glad they think this is a comedy. Still, never mind, I can turn that to my advantage; the boy's no fool, and I don't pity the maid who gets him. Now watch this; he's going to 'make conversation' with me. I'm sure I shall find it most instructive.

DORANT: What a striking girl. That profile would be a credit to any woman in Society; now to get better acquainted... Since we're bein' so familiar and the old formality's straight out the window, tell me something, Lisette, is your mistress anything like you? She must be quite a dazzler if she's got you for a maid.

SILVIA: Birmingham, this question would seem to indicate that you are now, as I understand is customary in these scenes, about to engage me in seductive conversation: is that correct?

DORANT: Good Lord no, that wasn't the plan at all. Though I am of course your typical chauffeur, I've never been much of a one for the maids; I've never cared much for the domestic banter, though of course in your case...well, that's quite a different matter. What! I'm quite overcome with you. Almost shy. I'm usually terrifically familiar but that doesn't seem the right tack with you somehow, I keep on wanting to take my hat off, and when I speak common with you I feel as though I'm just putting it on, in fact I feel instinctively as if I ought to treat you with respect: funny, really. What sort of a maid are you anyway, eh, you look like a real lady to me.

SILVIA: Oh dear, I seem to inspire precisely those same sentiments in every chauffeur I ever meet.

DORANT: And in every master too I'll bet.

SILVIA: What a well-rehearsed routine you have – but as I have already indicated, I am *not* susceptible to flattery from people with wardrobes like yours.

DORANT: Are you trying to say you don't like me in this uniform?

SILVIA: No, Birmingham. I'm not. Now, let's forget about love, and let's be friends.

DORANT: Is that all? The final line of your routine is grammatically correct but emotionally impossible.

SILVIA: (*Aside.*) What an extraordinary man for a chauffeur. Nevertheless, let us pursue that line; it was once foretold I should never get married except to a real gentleman; and

22

I promised not to listen to offers from any man who wasn't one.

DORANT: Good God! How extraordinary; I feel just the same way about women as you do about men; I've taken a vow never to get serious with any girl who isn't a real lady.

SILVIA: Now hardly seems the time to abandon such a lofty ideal.

DORANT: You never know, I might not be abandoning as much as one thinks; you're very distinguished-looking... perhaps you are of noble birth and know it not.

SILVIA: I would thank you for that moving little speech were it not made at the expense of my mother.

DORANT: Why not even the score with an insult aimed at mine? Or perhaps you don't think I'm distinguished-looking enough to be worth being rude to.

SILVIA: (*Aside.*) Oh you're worth it alright. But that's hardly the issue here: that's enough comic dialogue – I was promised a guaranteed gentleman and I won't settle for less.

DORANT: Lord, even if I was one, I'd find your prophecy a bit daunting: I'd be afraid of finding out I wasn't really who I thought I was. I don't believe in the stars. But I believe in your face.

SILVIA: (*Aside.*) He doesn't give up, does he? Have you quite finished? Since the stars excluded you from their calculations I don't think you should include them in yours.

DORANT: They never said I shouldn't love you.

SILVIA: No, but they did say that it wouldn't do you any good if you did, and I'm happy to be able to confirm their opinion.

DORANT: You're right of course, Lisette, Pride suits you perfectly. It was the one finishing touch you seemed to lack – I've been trying to work out what it was that was missing ever since I first saw you, and now that I've found it – though it plays hell with any plans I may have had – I can console myself with the knowledge that my loss is your gain.

SILVIA: (*Aside.*) Quite frankly, the boy's a surprise, though not an entirely pleasant one. Tell me, who are you, and where did you learn to talk like that?

DORANT: The son of a good family fallen on hard times.

SILVIA: Oh...well here's to good times just around the corner; I only wish there was something I could do... Lady Luck's been a bit rough on you, hasn't she?

DORANT: Cupid's been rougher; I'd rather have his permission to ask for your heart than all the tea in China.

SILVIA: (*Aside.*) Heavens, anyone would think we'd rehearsed this. Birmingham, I cannot bring myself to object to the manner of your conversation, but I would ask that we change the subject. How about...your master. You can not talk about Love, I take it.

DORANT: You could not inspire it.

SILVIA: Oh now I shall get cross. You're making me impatient. Change the subject.

DORANT: Change your face.

SILVIA: (*Aside.*) Actually I'm beginning to find him quite amusing. Well then, Birmingham, it seems you simply can't help yourself. In which case I shall be forced to leave you. Which I really should have done already.

DORANT: Wait, Lisette, there was something else I wanted to talk to you about. But I can't remember what it was.

SILVIA: Yes, I had something I wanted to talk to you about as well – but you've made me quite lose my thread too.

DORANT: I remember asking you if your mistress was anything like you – (*DORANT goes back a couple of pages and tries to start the scene again:*) Since we're being so familiar and the old formality's straight out the window, tell me something, Lisette, is your mistress as lovely as you are – any woman would be a fool to risk comparison with you –

SILVIA: Your brief detour has got you back on the same old track, goodbye.

DORANT: Oh, no, honestly – Lisette – this is about my master, really.

SILVIA: Good, I wanted to talk to you about him, I'd rather hoped you might be able to tell me, confidentially, what he's like. That you're attached to him predisposes me to like him; he can't be all bad if he's got you working for him.

DORANT: Could I please just say how kind it was of you to say that.

SILVIA: Would you please just ignore how foolish it was of me to say it.

DORANT: You see – it's the way you come out with these things that makes me feel...beside myself. Do as you please; I find you irresistible; and I find it most extraordinary that I am...in...servitude to one of the most adorable creatures I have ever met.

SILVIA: And I find it most odd that I'm prepared to listen to this sort of thing, because frankly, it's unlike me.

DORANT: You're right, the whole thing is unlikely.

SILVIA: (*Aside.*) It doesn't seem to matter what he says, I haven't gone, I am not going. I am still here, and I am still talking to him. Really, it's beyond a joke. Goodbye.

DORANT: Let's finish what we wanted to say.

SILVIA: Goodbye, I said; no more liberties. When your master gets here I'll try and find out the things my mistress wants to know about him by myself, if he seems worth the effort. If you want to wait for him that room there is yours.

DORANT: Good heavens, here comes my master now!
(*Enter ARLECCHINO.*)

ARLECCHINO: Ah! There you are, Birmingham! My suitcase and I, 'ave they been well received?

DORANT: It is hardly possible we should be other than well received in a house such as this, sir.

ARLECCHINO: Dinestars said, Do Go Orn Up, we'll inform your Farther In Lore and Waif that yoor 'ere.

SILVIA: You mean to say Mr Prowde and his daughter, sir, I'm sure.

ARLECCHINO: Eh? Yah, Farther in Lore, Waif, same thing. Get Engaged, Get Married, is all organised – Wedding? – A Mere Detail, What?

SILVIA: A Detail which requires some consideration, one would have thought.

ARLECCHINO: Yes, but once One has Thought Once About One's Marriage One Tends Never To Think About It Again Does One?

SILVIA: (*To DORANT.*) Apparently men of good family can be rather in-bred where you come from, Birmingham.

ARLECCHINO: And what are the staff saying, miss?

SILVIA: Nothing, I was just saying that I'll ask Mr Prowde to come down.

ARLECCHINO: Ah, yes, Farther In Lore.

SILVIA: He isn't, yet.

DORANT: She is right, sir – after all the marriage hasn't actually taken place yet.

ARLECCHINO: But One Has Come Specifically to Ensure that it Does.

DORANT: But you should still wait until it has –

ARLECCHINO: Good Heavens! Father in Law today, Father in Law tomorrow, what's the difference?

SILVIA: In fact there's hardly any difference between being married and not being married is there really, sir, so I'll just run off and tell your father-in-law that you're here.

ARLECCHINO: Don't forget the Waif. And tell me something, you pretty-little-thing-you…are you the…chambermaid… in this Hestablishment?

SILVIA: If you say so, sir.

ARLECCHINO: Oh good, That makes me very happy. Will the Famly Approve? Whaddyou think?

SILVIA: I think you're…terrifically amusing.

ARLECCHINO: Oh Good! I might take you up on that later…

SILVIA: And very becoming it is in you, sir, to be so modest about it. Now you must excuse me, downstairs must have forgotten to tell your father-in-law or I'm sure he'd be here by now, I'll go myself.

ARLECCHINO: Do say One is so Looking Forward to meeting him.

SILVIA: How very odd. Neither of these men know their proper place.
(*Exit SILVIA to search for MR PROWDE.*)

SCENE 8

ARLECCHINO: Eh, sir, not a bad entrance, eh? The maid fancies me already.

DORANT: Lout.

ARLECCHINO: What? I entered like a real gent.

DORANT: You made me a solemn promise you would desist from your ridiculous manner of speech. I coached you *exactly*. I gave you strict instructions to take the situation seriously. Well, I see now I was a fool to trust you.

ARLECCHINO: I get much better in the next scene. I will do The Serious; and if that doesn't do the trick, I'll do The Upset – and if it is really necessary, I'll even do The Cry!

DORANT: I don't know where I am with this any more; the whole thing's giving me a headache. What the hell am I going to do?

ARLECCHINO: The daughter's no good then?

DORANT: Oh do shut up!

(*Enter MR PROWDE and MAURICE.*)

This is Mr Prowde.

SCENE 9

PROWDE: My dear sir, a thousand apologies for having kept you waiting – they've only just told me that you're here.

ARLECCHINO: My Dear Sir, a Thizand? Surely Nought; One Mistake, One Apology – but Anyway, Do 'elp yourself to as many of Main as you want.

PROWDE: I shall attempt to ensure that I have no further need of them.

ARLECCHINO: I am, Sir, At Your Service. No, I mean I am not Sir, at your service, I am NOT a servant, no, yes, master, servant etc, etc.

PROWDE: Anyway, I'm delighted to meet you – I've been so looking forward to it.

ARLECCHINO: Of Coarse One would have come Orn earlier with Birmingham here but when One has been Travelling One knows Wart a State One gets into and One simply felt uneasy Bite presenting Oneself before One had had Time to change into something a little more...Tastier.

MAURICE: The desired effect has been achieved.

PROWDE: Quite. My daughter's just dressing; she's been feeling a little unwell – while we're waiting for her to come down, may I offer you a little refreshment?

ARLECCHINO: Oh, One will drink with anybody.

(*There is a problem with the refreshments: LISETTE is still dressing; DORANT doesn't know what a butler really does, and SILVIA certainly isn't fetching ARLECCHINO a drink. So MR PROWDE rings the bell in vain... Anyway, eventually somehow the drinks get served.*)

PROWDE: Birmingham – my dear boy – do have a glass yourself.

ARLECCHINO: Used to drinking the Best you know this Fellow. Got Quite a taste for the Finer Things in Life.

PROWDE: Well I hope he'll feel free to indulge it.

(*The Four Men Have a Drink. LISETTE makes her Big Entrance dressed as SILVIA. The Men React. SILVIA, watching from the wings, sees 'herself'. MAURICE sings a song about Love.*)

Act Two

SCENE 1

(*Afternoon.*

SILVIA has met DORANT, LISETTE has met ARLECCHINO; the game has begun. How is it going?

MR PROWDE is alone on stage. Enter LISETTE.)

PROWDE: And what can I do for you, Lisette?

LISETTE: I have to see you for a minute.

PROWDE: What about?

LISETTE: I thought you ought to know how it's going so you're not in the dark and I won't be to blame.

PROWDE: This all sounds very serious.

LISETTE: Yes very serious. You gave Miss Silvia permission to get dressed up, well at the time I didn't think there was any harm in it either, and I was wrong wasn't I.

PROWDE: And what harm is there in it now?

LISETTE: Well Sir, far be it from me to blow my own trumpet but; it sounds improper I know but I have to tell you that if you don't take a firm hand this son-in-law you've organised isn't going to have anything left to give the Mistress your daughter on her wedding day, and I think she should tell him who she really is now, as a matter of some urgency; if she waits till tomorrow morning well then I shan't be held responsible.

PROWDE: And what makes you think he wouldn't still want her, after he knew who she really was? Aren't you rather underestimating her powers of attraction?

LISETTE: No Sir but you're not estimating mine enough. They're having their wicked way and I'm advising you not to let them get away with it.
(*MR PROWDE laughs.*)

PROWDE: Please accept my heartiest congratulations, Lisette.

LISETTE: Well there we are then, very amusing sir I'm sure, the joke's on me, but I'm sorry, it's you who's going to get sent the bill.

PROWDE: That really need not concern you, Lisette; you just carry on.

LISETTE: Alright I'll say it again. He isn't wasting any time. At lunch he said he liked me, at dinner he'll tell me he loves me and by tomorrow morning I expect he'll be offering me adoration on a permanent basis. It's all in the worst possible taste, a girl like me doesn't deserve it, you can say what you like, that doesn't mean it's not happening. You do see what I mean. By this time tomorrow I'll have been adored.

PROWDE: I don't see why you should find that a problem. If he loves you that much, I expect he'll marry you.

LISETTE: What! You'd stop it.

PROWDE: No, I wouldn't – I give you my word as a gentleman – if you can get him to go that far –

LISETTE: I'm warning you, sir. Up to this point I have done nothing to enhance my natural assets, I've just let them get on with it, and he's already hotting up. If I set to work, he'll boil over, and then that will be that.

PROWDE: Boil, poach, scramble and then marry him with my blessing – if you think you can.

LISETTE: I think I'm going to be a very rich girl.

PROWDE: Oh and by the way, has my daughter spoken to you at all? What does *she* make of her intended?

LISETTE: Well we hardly have a moment to talk about it really, seeing as how he never leaves me alone. But I should say, from the look of things, she's not best pleased. Put out. I'm just waiting for her to tell me to get rid of him.

PROWDE: Now that I forbid you to do. I am also avoiding talking to her – I have my own reasons for prolonging the proceedings – I want her to have plenty of time to make up her mind about her future husband. And how is the chauffeur behaving himself? Not entertaining any ideas about my daughter I hope?

LISETTE: He's a funny one. Comes on very grand with her I've noticed, fancies himself. Looks at her and sighs a lot.

PROWDE: And does she mind?

LISETTE: No…but she does blush.

PROWDE: Good – surely not; it takes more than a sighing chauffeur to embarrass her.

LISETTE: She's blushing.

PROWDE: With indignation, I expect.

LISETTE: Yes I expect that's it.

PROWDE: Anyway when you do get a chance to talk to her I want you to tell her that you suspect the chauffeur of trying to prejudice her against his master – and if she gets upset, don't let it concern you – that's my lookout.

SCENE 2

(*Enter ARLECCHINO.*)

PROWDE: I take it Mr Dorant here is looking for you.

ARLECCHINO: Ah, there you are, [you fabulous creature you]; I 'ave enquired after you all over. At Your Service, Dear Farther In Lore Practically Anyway.

PROWDE: At yours. Well, I'll leave you two alone together. I approve of you young people getting to know each other a bit before you get married.

ARLECCHINO: One would be Quite Happy to do the Two Jobs At Once.

PROWDE: Now let's not get too hasty. Good afternoon.

(*Exit MR PROWDE.*)

SCENE 3

ARLECCHINO: Madam, High Ham Hinstructed not to get too Hasty. High Ham 'Owever of the Hopinion that 'Aste is only Inappropriate in the Hold.

LISETTE: I can scarce believe Patience should be such a Trial, Sir, and think you play th'Impatient out of Gallantry merely – after all you have only just got here. A love so newly born as yours can scarcely be so Lusty an Infant.

ARLECCHINO: Ah, there you're wrong, oh wonder of the age – A love such as mine cannot idle in the cradle. The first time I saw you, he sprang into life. The second, he started to grow Up. [The third], he is a Big Boy... [Mother! Take care of your Child!]

LISETTE: Once he's big enough to go out to work I'm sure I can help you find him a suitable position. I should hate people to think that I lack maternal instincts.

ARLECCHINO: Perhaps until such time as he gets on the job you could offer him your lily-white hand to keep him amused.

LISETTE: There we are then, oh what a greedy little boy we are, I can see Mummy and Daddy aren't going to get a moment's peace unless you're kept happy.

ARLECCHINO: [Little darling baby's-rattle of my soul! You refresh those parts other beers cannot reach!]

LISETTE: That's enough, let's not be too greedy.

ARLECCHINO: [But I'm still thirsty etc etc.]

LISETTE: Now now, let's be reasonable.

ARLECCHINO: [Reason! Ohime! I have lost it. Your darling eyes have stolen it!]

LISETTE: But is't possible you should love me so much? I find it scarcely credible.

ARLECCHINO: Credible, incredible – let's not worry about that – I love you – madly! Why do I love you? – *Regardez dans votre miroir…*

LISETTE: I rather think *mon miroir* would only remind me of how unlikely the whole situation is.

ARLECCHINO: [Ah! What an adorable little darling!] Madam, Your Modesty is but Hypocrisy…

(*LISETTE and ARLECCHINO are just about to investigate the whole issue of Modesty and Hypocrisy when there is a knock on the door –*)

LISETTE: Someone's coming.

SCENE 4

(*Enter DORANT.*)

DORANT: Excuse me sir, could I see you for a moment.

ARLECCHINO: No! [Curse Him!] (*To LISETTE.*) Servants!! Nought a Moment's Peace!

LISETTE: Oh do see what he wants.

DORANT: Just one word, sir.

ARLECCHINO: Madam, if he attempts Two, the Third will be 'You Are', and the Fourth, 'Fired'. [Do excuse me.]

DORANT: Come over here, idiot. (*He hits him.*)

ARLECCHINO: [You said one word, not one smack –] (*To LISETTE.*) My Queen, do excuse me.

LISETTE: Oh by all means.

DORANT: Now just you stop all this at once or you'll give the game away; you're supposed to be being serious, sensitive and a little distressed; are you listening to me?

ARLECCHINO: [Yes yes I'm listening; don't you worry and now clear off.] (*DORANT is amazed by this far too idiomatic rendering of the line, so ARLECCHINO says it again in a different style in order to get him to go.*) Quite, Quite, Nothing to Worry About, That will be All.

(*Exit DORANT.*)

SCENE 5

ARLECCHINO: [Now, where was I...ah, yes...] Madam, Before we were so rudely interrupted... High was A Bite to say... Something, refained. But now...high fained my mained is come over all Common, on account of my love, which is so very extraordinary... And speaking of Love, do you think yours feels like sitting over here with mine?

LISETTE: Let us hope that one day it will.

ARLECCHINO: Will it be long?

LISETTE: What a very direct question; I'm almost embarrassed –

ARLECCHINO: [What do you expect: when a man is on fire, he has to call for the fire brigade!!]

LISETTE: Though of course were it socially acceptable for a woman in my position to speak frankly of what she really feels inside –

ARLECCHINO: [Please feel free to he absolutely frank –]

LISETTE: But sadly the modesty of my sex forbids it –

ARLECCHINO: [I had heard that modesty was going out of fashion these days –]

LISETTE: What are you asking me to do!

ARLECCHINO: [Tell me a little that you love me. Listen:] High Love You. [Repeat after me:] High Love You... [Princess; come on...] High Love You etc. etc.

LISETTE: Oh you insatiable beast! (*They play the repeating game together until finally LISETTE says:*) I love you!

ARLECCHINO: (*Climbing the walls.*) [Oh! I'm dying! I'm going crazy! I think I'm going to have to climb the walls!!] HUE LOVE ME!!!

LISETTE: I must confess myself a little alarmed by the sudden onset of this devotion. Don't you ever worry that one might love someone less once one gets to know them better?

ARLECCHINO: Ah! Madam –

LISETTE: You think I'm the perfect Lady, but, for instance, I might not be at all...

ARLECCHINO: [And you think I'm a perfect Gentleman.]

LISETTE: After all I am not the Mistress...of my own fate –

ARLECCHINO: [And I am not the Master –]

LISETTE: Although speaking for myself I am sure I should have been attracted to you whatever class of person you'd been –

ARLECCHINO: (*Who by this time is grovelling, beginning his build up to full prostration at the end of the scene.*) [Be attracted to me! Be attracted to me!]

LISETTE: May I flatter myself to think that you feel just the same way about me?

ARLECCHINO: Signora, if when I first saw you you had been the – [how do you say it] – the Maid! – you would still be *la mia principessa.*

LISETTE: Let's hope you'll always feel the same way about me.

ARLECCHINO: Let us do more than hope; let us swear –

LISETTE: – to love one another for ever, disregarding any minor violations of the agreed rules of socially acceptable behaviour which you may or may not find yourself inspired to commit on my behalf –

ARLECCHINO: *Sì.*

LISETTE: I couldn't agree more.

ARLECCHINO: [Your kindness overwhelms me and I prostrate myself before it.]

LISETTE: Oh no please. I can't possibly bear to look at you in that position. It was silly of me to have let you. Do get up.

(*There is of course a knock on the door.*)
There's somebody coming again.

SCENE 6

(*Enter SILVIA.*)
LISETTE: What do you want, Lisette?
SILVIA: I have to talk to you, madam.
ARLECCHINO: (*To LISETTE.*) [Wouldn't you know it!] (*To
    SILVIA.*) Sweetheart... (*He gives her a big tip.*) Fifteen
    minutes... (*SILVIA refuses to leave.*) Wear High Come Frorm,
    Maids Honely Come Hwen Their Corled.
SILVIA: Beggin' your pardon sir but I have to speak to Madam.
ARLECCHINO: [What a stubborn maid.] (*To LISETTE.*) [Queen
    of my life...get her off!] (*To SILVIA.*) That Will Be Hall!
    Listen, he told us to get to know each other before we got
    married, now can't you see we're busy.
LISETTE: Perhaps you could come back in a short while,
    Lisette.
SILVIA: Yes Ma'am, but –
ARLECCHINO: (*Losing his temper.*) [But! But! But excuse me for
    getting so angry!]
SILVIA: What a revolting man. I'm sorry Ma'am but the matter
    is rather pressing.
LISETTE: (*To ARLECCHINO.*) Would you excuse me?
ARLECCHINO: [Oh no, excuse me, I must be patient, I must
    just go for a little walk while she takes her time saying
    what she has to say.] One Simply Can't get The Staff These
    Days.
    (*Exit ARLECCHINO.*)

SCENE 7

SILVIA: Well, I think it's utterly charming of you to have
    dismissed him so promptly and thus spared me the
    indignity of being in the same room at the same time as
    that *beast.*
LISETTE: 'Scuse me, madam, but I can't do two parts at once
    here; either I'm maiding or I'm mistressing.

SILVIA: Quite; and now that he is no longer with us you will, when I say that I must speak with you, kindly respond as a Maid. It must be quite clear to you that this man isn't at all suitable –

LISETTE: You haven't had time to examine him all over yet.

SILVIA: Examine him? Need one look twice in order to see how unsuitable he is? He's quite simply out of the question. Apparently my father doesn't share my repugnance; he's deliberately avoiding me. Since that is the case, I shall have to rely on you to extricate me from this delicate situation by discreetly suggesting to this gentleman that you are *not* inclined to accept his kind offer of marriage.

LISETTE: I couldn't do that, madam.

SILVIA: You couldn't. And why not?

LISETTE: Your father has forbidden me.

SILVIA: That doesn't sound like Father. Forbidding anything is usually quite outside his range.

LISETTE: Absolutely forbidden me.

SILVIA: Well perhaps you would be so kind as to inform him of my aversion and assure him that it's definite; when you have, he won't want to pursue this any further.

LISETTE: 'Scuse me for asking, madam, but what is it about this fiancé that's so revolting exactly?

SILVIA: I told you, I don't care for him. And I don't much care for your attitude either.

LISETTE: You just need the time to get to really know him, that's all.

SILVIA: I disliked him quite enough on superficial acquaintance not to want to spend any time getting to dislike him intimately.

LISETTE: His chauffeur, the one with the manners, he hasn't said anything to make you think like that about him?

SILVIA: The last thing we need in this situation is a chauffeur.

LISETTE: It's just I shouldn't trust him, too much of a way with his words.

SILVIA: Now please don't start with one of your thumbnail personality sketches, we can do without them. I have only allowed the chauffeur to engage me in the barest minimum of conversation, but I must say I found the few words he did exchange with me remarkably perceptive.

LISETTE: I think he looks just the sort who'd make unsuitable remarks to show off how clever he was.

SILVIA: Well one is rather exposed to comment, dressed like this. What exactly are you driving at? Where on earth did you get the preposterous idea that this boy is the reason why I loathe his master, when he has got nothing to do with it. And yes, alright, I did make a fool of myself listening to his stories but that is no reason to get him into trouble with his employer or to make him out to be some sort of double dealer or fraud.

LISETTE: Well madam, if we're going to adopt that tone in his defence and if we're going to upset ourselves then I've nothing more to say on the matter I'm sure.

SILVIA: If I'm going to adopt what tone in his defence? And what about your tone? What are you trying to imply? Are you hinting at something?

LISETTE: I was merely saying, madam, that I've never seen you in such a state and I can't think what I've done to be spoken to so sharply. And if the chauffeur didn't say anything, well, that's alright then, there's no need for you to get so worked up on his behalf, I believe you, there's an end to the matter and far be it from me to take against someone you were carrying a torch for I'm sure.

SILVIA: There you are you see that is exactly the sort of thing I have to put up with, twisting and turning every word I say. It makes me all so vexed, I could quite frankly cry.

LISETTE: Why's that then, madam? I hope you're not reading double meanings into things.

SILVIA: Oh so now I'm reading double meanings. I'm getting worked up on his behalf. I'm carrying a torch. Carrying a torch dear God. Me, carry a torch. Have *all* the rules of normal behaviour been suspended? What on earth do you expect me to say, what am I to presume that you mean, where do you think we are and just who exactly do you think you're talking to?

LISETTE: I really couldn't say. It'll take me a while to recover my poise. How very surprising.

(*Exit LISETTE.*)

SILVIA: She sometimes has a way of putting things that can make one feel quite...out of character. Thank you. You may go now. I find you quite intolerable. I should rather be on my own. I can manage.

(*SILVIA alone.*

Music.)

SCENE 8

Chase Number One

(*The rules:*

- *DORANT must find SILVIA.*
- *SILVIA must be alone; SILVIA must avoid ARLECCHINO.*
- *LISETTE must get to work on ARLECCHINO.*
- *ARLECCHINO must find LISETTE.*
- *MR PROWDE must avoid SILVIA but at the same time keep an eye on her.*
- *MAURICE must amuse himself.*

During the chase, people rehearse fragments of text for their forthcoming scenes. LISETTE quick-changes her way through four increasingly effective frocks. The chase must climax with LISETTE and ARLECCHINO almost managing to get together, but being prevented by SILVIA.

DORANT texts:)

1 Lisette, I – Lisette I want to – Lisette I have to, I really have to –

2 Lisette, notwithstanding the distance you feel there is between us – Lisette – notwithstanding the fact that you hold yourself so distant from me, that you keep yourself to yourself – that you are somehow –

3 Lisette, though you're keeping your distance yet I feel myself bound to talk to you, I find myself talking to you even when we're apart, even when you're not there I feel –

4 Lisette I know you're trying to avoid me but I have to talk to you.

(*SILVIA texts:*)

1 I am still shaking from that last scene. The sheer insolence with which the staff assume one shares their below-stairs attitudes. They drag one down to their level. I have tried to calm down but I'm sorry I can't. I daren't even think of some of the expressions she used or I'll set myself off again. After all, it's a chauffeur we're talking about. A chauffeur. Really!

2 A chauffeur. It's inconceivable. The mere suggestion is horrible and I shall dismiss it from my mind. And I shan't take it out on him.

3 Well it isn't his fault. After all, it's a chauffeur we're talking about. Really. The mere suggestion. I mean look at him, that is what I'm getting myself into such a state over. Well it's not his fault the poor boy and I mustn't take it out on him.

SCENE 9

DORANT: Lisette – I know you're trying to keep your distance but really, I must speak to you – I have a complaint to make.

SILVIA: Birmingham, don't let's be too familiar, please.

DORANT: If you like, I won't be.

SILVIA: I don't. But you are being.

DORANT: So are you then. You said 'Please'.

SILVIA: Words sometimes fail me.

DORANT: It seems a pity to waste what little time we have left in each other's company in formalities.

SILVIA: Oh, is your master leaving? Not that I'd mind if he was –

DORANT: Nor if I was. I was just finishing your line for you.

SILVIA: I am quite capable of finishing my own lines when I want to. You never entered my head.

DORANT: I can't get you out of mine.

SILVIA: Listen, Birmingham, and this is the last time I'll say this, stay, leave, come back, I really shouldn't mind which you do and I don't, I don't care one way or the other, I don't hate you, and I don't love you – and I won't ever love you, at least not unless I go completely mad. That's the way I feel, it would be quite unreasonable of me to feel any other way, and it's only fair I tell you as much.

DORANT: I am unimaginably unhappy. I rather think you may have ruined my life.

SILVIA: What on earth did he think was going on – oh the poor boy – Now get a hold of yourself. You're talking to me, I'm talking to you, and that's quite enough, in fact it's a little too much, believe you me, and if you were a little more experienced in these things – I mean – if you understood what was really going on – you'd understand that I'm just doing what's proper: you'd realise that I'm only acting out of the kindness of my heart, in fact if I saw another woman being this kind I'd tell her she was making a fool of herself; not that I feel a fool, because I know that what I'm doing is right. Now as I say I'm only telling you all this in order to be kind, and I must stop now, that sort of kindness is all very well in the heat of the moment but I'm not the sort of woman who can keep on reassuring herself of the innocence of her intentions all night and so really, in the end, the whole thing doesn't make any sense. So let's just stop all this shall we, just stop it, Birmingham. Please. After all, what's the point, it's a joke, so, I really think that's all there is to say.

DORANT: Lisette, do you have any idea of how much pain I'm in?

SILVIA: Now, you had something you wanted to say to me; you came in, and you said you had a complaint to make; well, about what?

(*DORANT goes out and attempts to replay the scene from the top. Enter DORANT.*)

DORANT: Lisette I know you're trying to keep your distance but really…really I must speak to you Lisette I have a complaint to make – oh it was nothing, nothing at all really. I just wanted to look at you and it seemed like a good excuse.

SILVIA: What can I say? I've tried being strict and it gets me nowhere.

(*DORANT tries again.*)

DORANT: Lisette I have to talk to you. I have a complaint
to make. Your mistress has accused me of speaking
disparagingly about my master to you.

SILVIA: Well she's imagining it, and if she accuses you again
you should tell her as much straight out and then leave me
to deal with her...

DORANT: Actually that wasn't it.

SILVIA: Well if that's all you had to say then I think that's the
end of this scene.

(*SILVIA goes to exit, but:*)

DORANT: Please let me at least look at you.

SILVIA: Now that is a good reason for me to stay. I am to
arouse passion in Birmingham. One day I am going to look
back at all this and I am going to laugh.

DORANT: You're right, this is a complete farce, I don't know
what I'm saying or what I want from you. Goodbye.

(*DORANT makes an exit, but:*)

SILVIA: Goodbye, yes, I'm sure that's for the best – but,
speaking of goodbyes, there is just one thing I'd like to
know. Your master and you are leaving, you said, was that
bit serious?

DORANT: If I don't leave then I shall go mad.

SILVIA: That wasn't the answer I was hoping for.

DORANT: And my biggest mistake was not leaving the
moment I met you.

SILVIA: I must remember to forget every single thing he says.

DORANT: If you only knew, Lisette, what an odd situation
I'm in.

SILVIA: Not half so odd as mine, I assure you.

DORANT: What have I done wrong? It's not as if I've made
myself attractive.

SILVIA: Oh no of course not.

DORANT: – and anyway what good would it do me to try and
make you love me. Even if you were to fall in love –

SILVIA: From which fate Heaven preserve me. And if I did,
you wouldn't even notice. I'd do it so well I wouldn't even
know I'd done it myself. Really, the very idea.

DORANT: It is really true then, that you don't hate me, you don't love me, and you won't ever love me?

SILVIA: There's no question.

DORANT: I have one. What makes me such an appalling prospect?

SILVIA: Nothing; you're not the problem.

DORANT: Alright then. Say 'I won't ever love you' a hundred times.

SILVIA: Oh I think once was enough. You have to try to believe that I mean what I say.

DORANT: You're right. I have to. So, make my reckless passion pointless; save me from it, tell me I'm a fool to fear its consequences; you *don't* hate me, you *don't* love me, you won't *ever* love me, go on, make it drown out the beating of my frantic heart, because believe me, I am trying, but I'm struggling, I'm struggling with myself, and I need your help; I'm on my knees.

(*And he is. Enter MR PROWDE and MAURICE.*)

SCENE 10

SILVIA: Oh of course. I should have known we'd end up in this position. God I feel a fool. It's my fault he's down there. Do get up now Birmingham, please. Someone might come in. I'll say whatever you want. What would you like me to say? 'I don't hate you.' 'At all.' – Now do get up. 'I would love you, if I could.' 'I don't not like you.' – Really that's the best I can do.

DORANT: What? Lisette, if I wasn't who I am, if I was rich, if I was a gentleman and if I loved you as much as I do love you, do you think you wouldn't find me quite as unattractive as you do?

SILVIA: Definitely –

DORANT: You wouldn't hate me. You'd put up with me.

SILVIA: Gladly. But you would have to get up.

DORANT: You said that as if you meant it and if you did then I think I shall go mad.

SILVIA: I'm saying everything you want me to say and you're still not getting up.

PROWDE: It seems a shame to interrupt you; you are doing well my dears – bravo!

SILVIA: I did try and stop him getting on his knees, sir. But then you can hardly be telling people what they can do and what they can't do when you're in my position, can you?

PROWDE: I should say both of you were in exactly the right position – but we did want to have just a word, Lisette – you can pick up where you left off after we've gone – is that alright with you, Birmingham?

DORANT: I'll be going now, sir.

PROWDE: Do. Oh, and do try and speak of your master with a little more discretion in future.

DORANT: Me, sir?

MAURICE: You sir, Birmingham; people do say that respect for your employers is not your most outstanding feature.

DORANT: I don't know what they mean.

PROWDE: Thank you – thank you. You can explain yourself on another occasion.

(*Exit DORANT.*)

SCENE 11

PROWDE: Well, Silvia, you don't seem able to look at us, you look almost flustered –

SILVIA: Do I, Father? And what have I got to be flustered about? I am feeling quite myself, thank God.

MAURICE: But there is definitely something going on, sister.

SILVIA: In your mind, possibly, brother dear, but in mine there is nothing 'going on' except astonishment at your suggestion that there might be.

PROWDE: Was that boy who's just left the one who has inspired this violent antipathy towards his master?

SILVIA: Who – Dorant's man?

MAURICE: The dashing Birmingham.

SILVIA: If Birmingham is dashing it is news to me, and no, it wasn't, because he never talks to me about his master.

PROWDE: Oh, I was told that it was he who'd been putting you off – and that was rather what I wanted to talk to you about –

SILVIA: There really wouldn't be any point, Father; the only person who has inspired my natural aversion for his master is his master.

MAURICE: How right you are, sister.

SILVIA: You make it all sound very mysterious.

MAURICE: Nerves, sister? You *are* in a state.

SILVIA: Because I am sick and I am tired of wearing this costume and if my father doesn't mind I would like to take it off now.

PROWDE: Not just yet, daughter. That's actually what I wanted to talk to you about. Since I was good enough to permit you your charade you will, if you don't mind, be good enough to suspend your judgement on Mr Dorant and to discover for yourself whether the opinion others have given you of him is correct.

SILVIA: You're really not listening to me are you? No one has given me any opinion.

MAURICE: Our over-talkative chauffeur hasn't made you feel a little squeamish about him?

SILVIA: What an objectionable way of putting it. 'Squeamish'. 'Squeamish about him'. I seem suddenly to find myself surrounded on all sides by the most curious turns of phrase; deafened by the clash of infelicitous verb against inappropriate epithet. First I'm 'flustered', then something's 'up', and now I'm being made 'squeamish' by someone 'dashing'. All of which may make perfect sense to you but I don't understand a word.

MAURICE: I rather think it's you who are the curious turn. With whom, exactly, are you so angry; and why, exactly, are you being so defensive; and do you realise under what suspicions you are in danger of falling?

SILVIA: Never mind, brother. I'm sure it's simply bad luck that I find your vocabulary so grating this evening. Or is it that you're having one of your headaches; which suspicion exactly would you like me to fall under?

MAURICE: I must say you don't seem quite yourself to me either. I can only assume this is exactly the sort of outburst to which Lisette was referring. She simply enquired, she said, whether this chauffeur had spoken ill of his master to you and 'Madam,' as she put it, 'spoke up for him with such a passion that I am still all of a surprise' – we reprimanded her for this verbal infelicity – but then servants often don't quite know what they are saying.

SILVIA: How dare she. That girl is getting absolutely impossible. I was merely defending the boy against a patently unjust accusation.

MAURICE: An entirely natural impulse.

SILVIA: (*To MAURICE.*) Quite. Just because I am naturally fair-minded, because I don't like to see anybody getting hurt, because I wanted to save a servant from getting into his master's bad books, I'm described as having outbursts, losing my temper – which of course makes me completely surprising. Two seconds later one of the staff starts gossiping, naturally one gets annoyed, one tries to shut her up, one points out the merits of one's case – and she was the one who started it – my *case* – I suppose I had better prepare my defence now had I, acquire some alibis, make sure my evidence isn't open to misinterpretation. I stand accused. Well, of what – well do tell me somebody in case the charge is serious – or are we just joking – are we just making me a joke? I'm very upset.

PROWDE: Gently does it.

SILVIA: Gentleness has nothing to do with it. Surprises, consequences, why can't people just say what they mean. Someone accused the chauffeur, did they? Well they were wrong. You're wrong, Lisette's ridiculous, he's innocent, I've had enough. I don't know why we're still talking about it. Now I really am upset.

PROWDE: There's really no need to be so restrained, daughter. Perhaps you would like to speak your mind to me as well? Still, I'm sure we can do more than just talk about it. It's clear that the only suspect in the case is the chauffeur: Dorant will just have to send him away.

SILVIA: This ridiculous disguise. Don't let Lisette anywhere near me, I loathe her. Even more than I loathe this Dorant.

PROWDE: I'm sure you needn't see her unless you want to; but you ought to be delighted the boy's going, he's obviously fallen for you, which must be most annoying.

SILVIA: It doesn't bother me actually; he thinks I'm a maid and so that's how he talks to me – mind you, I don't let him just say what he likes, I keep a tight rein.

MAURICE: You're not quite as much the mistress of the situation as you say.

PROWDE: Didn't we just see him get down on his knees when you'd told him not to? And weren't you obliged to tell him that you didn't not like him before he'd get up off them? (*SILVIA chokes.*)

MAURICE: And furthermore, were you not, when he asked you whether you might one day love him, heard to tenderly utter the word 'gladly'? – without which word, one might conjecture, he might still be here.

SILVIA: Thank you for that learned summing-up, brother. But since I found the original incident unpleasant, I don't find the reprise very amusing either; and on that note, let's be serious for a moment. When is this comedy which seems to be being played at my expense, going to end?

PROWDE: I'm only asking that you don't decide to refuse him until you're in full possession of the facts. Give it just a little longer; you'll thank me for delaying the proceedings – I promise you.

MAURICE: I predict that you'll end up marrying this Dorant – and gladly… But Father, I would advocate clemency for the chauffeur.

SILVIA: Why? Personally I'll be glad to see him gone.

PROWDE: Let's leave it up to his master, shall we? (*Exit MR PROWDE.*)

MAURICE: No hard feelings.
(*Music.*
SILVIA as if alone.
Exit MAURICE.)

SCENE 12

SILVIA: (*Seems to have a sudden palpitation.*) Oh dear, what is the matter with my heart! I don't know if this is just embarrassment or what – the whole situation seems so fraught – I can't trust anyone. I don't like anyone. I don't like myself.

(*Enter DORANT unseen.*)

DORANT: Ah! I was looking for you, Lisette.

SILVIA: Well I wasn't worth finding because I don't want to see you.

(*She goes to exit.*)

DORANT: Don't go, Lisette, there's one final thing I have to say to you – it's something important, about your employers.

SILVIA: Go and say it to them then; every time I see you, you upset me; now do leave me alone.

DORANT: I could say the same thing – but – do listen – really – what I have to say will make everything different.

SILVIA: Alright then say it; I'm listening – I have been given strict instructions that my patience with you must be endless.

DORANT: Can you keep a secret?

SILVIA: I have never betrayed anyone.

DORANT: I wouldn't be confiding in you like this if I didn't respect you so much.

SILVIA: I'm sure you wouldn't, but do try and respect me without telling me about it, or I shall think this is another one of your good excuses.

DORANT: It isn't, Lisette. You promised to keep this secret… so, let's get to the point shall we… You've seen me at my most wretched: I love you, I can't stop myself from saying it –

SILVIA: Well I can stop myself from listening to it. Goodbye.

DORANT: Wait. This isn't Birmingham speaking to you any more.

SILVIA: Oh really and who is it then?

DORANT: Lisette, now you'll see what sort of a mill my heart has been through.

SILVIA: It's not your heart I'm talking to, it's you.

DORANT: Is anyone coming?

SILVIA: No.

DORANT: I've got to tell you, because of the mess things've got into; I'm too much of a decent sort really to let them carry on as they are.

SILVIA: Well?

DORANT: I think you should know the man who is with your mistress isn't who you think he is.

SILVIA: Who is he then?

DORANT: A chauffeur.

SILVIA: And.

DORANT: It's me who's Dorant.

SILVIA: (*Aside.*) Ah! Now I see how my heart works.

DORANT: I dressed up like this because I wanted to find out a bit about your mistress before getting engaged to her. It was all done with my father's consent – and now it's all turned into some dreadful dream. I hate the mistress who I was supposed to be marrying and I love the maid, who wasn't supposed to be anything except...the maid. What am I going to do? And I'm sorry to have to tell you this but your mistress has such poor taste in men that she's taken up with my chauffeur – to the point where she'd marry him if she could –

(*SILVIA stops him talking by kissing him. Then she turns to the audience:*)

SILVIA: I'm not going to tell him who I am.

INTERVAL

The action continues from exactly the point where it ended; SILVIA is kissing DORANT.

SILVIA: Well, what a novel situation you're in! Oh Sir, may I straightway offer my humble apologies if any remarks what have slipped into our conversations earlier have been at all irregular.

DORANT: Oh do shut up, Lisette, I can't stand it if yo
apologising, it reminds me of all that keeps us ap;
can't bear that.

SILVIA: You serious about me then? How much d'yo
me?

DORANT: Well obviously someone like me can't marry
someone like you – but enough not to want to have an
affair with anybody else – I'd be happy staying single,
knowing that you...'don't hate me'.

SILVIA: Since your heart has stooped so low as to notice me in
my present condition, it would seem the least I can do is
reciprocate. Which I would gladly do, were I not afraid of
the possible consequences.

DORANT: Couldn't you just look like a lady, Lisette, without
having to add speaking like one to your list of attractions?

SILVIA: Someone's coming! Don't do anything hasty about
your chauffeur – there's no rush – we'll see each other
again soon – I'm sure we'll be able to work something
out –

DORANT: Whatever you say –

(*Exit DORANT.*)

SILVIA: Well, I wonder what I would have done if it hadn't
been him.

SCENE 13

(*A small flurry of doors; ARLECCHINO, LISETTE, MAURICE.*)

MAURICE: I thought I'd better come and find you – we left
you in such a state I was quite worried about you; I'm sure
I can help, now listen –

SILVIA: There's some rather wonderful news. Everything's
different.

MAURICE: What is?

SILVIA: It isn't Birmingham at all, it's Dorant.

MAURICE: What are you talking about?

SILVIA: About him, I just found out, he's gone now, he told me
so himself.

MAURICE: Who did?

SILVIA: Didn't you hear what I said?

MAURICE: Yes but I'm blowed if I understood it.

SILVIA: Right, let's go; we must find Father, he really ought to know. I'll need your help too – I've just had an idea; pretend to be in love with me – I mean you've already hinted that you are, as a joke – but above all, don't give the game away.

MAURICE: How can I when I don't know what we're playing at?

SILVIA: So, brother dear, off we go; there's not a moment to lose. Nothing like this has happened to anybody ever. (*Exit SILVIA.*)

MAURICE: I do hope no one's going to become hysterical.
MAURICE sings a song about Love.

Chase Number Two

(*The rules:*

– MAURICE and MR PROWDE have to keep a much closer eye on things because they are moving that much faster.

– ARLECCHINO and LISETTE are getting pretty desperate.

– SILVIA is looking for her father.

– DORANT is nearly suicidal, and must avoid everyone but especially LISETTE.

MAURICE, having finished his song, announces, 'The Same, After Dinner'. Exit MAURICE.)

Act Three

SCENE 1

ARLECCHINO: Ah! Monsieur, Sir, [Sir my most highly respected master I beg of you, I implore you etc etc…]

DORANT: Yes!!

ARLECCHINO: 'Pity a poor man, sir, don't snatch away 'is only chance of 'appiness just when it's within 'is grasp!'

DORANT: That's enough, d'you think I can't tell when you're trying to make a fool out of me? You deserve a bloody good hiding.

ARLECCHINO: I do, I do, you're right, who am I to refuse what I have deserved, would you like me to go and get the stick? And when I have had it, the bloody good, can I go and deserve it some more?

DORANT: I've had enough of your cheek.

ARLECCHINO: [I may be a] cheek; [but I am also going to be a rich] cheek.

DORANT: It's sad really. Idiot!

ARLECCHINO: [That's okay, if you are a] cheek [then you don't mind being called an] idiot. [But remember, sir;] rich people marry idiots.

DORANT: Don't be so insolent – now, let me get this right; you want me to be party to the deception of a respectable household, and to allow you to marry the daughter of that household while pretending to be me? Listen; if you even mention this gross impertinence again, no sooner shall I have informed our host who you really are than I shall give you your notice.

ARLECCHINO: *Aspetto. La Madame,* [she loves me. She adores me.] *Si* – if I say to her, '*io sono – le chauffeur*'; and, she says, '[That is not a problem,] High Still Love Hue.' – Well? – (*ARLECCHINO plays or sings 'Here Comes the Bride'*.)

DORANT: If she finds out who you really are then I don't think I shall really care what happens.

ARLECCHINO: [Good!] I shall [immediately] disabuse this [generous young person] as to the significance of my usual accoutrements. I trust that a few brass buttons will not suffice to come between us, and that Love will see fit to usher me into The Drawing Room, even though Life has consigned me to The Garage.

(*Exit ARLECCHINO.*)

SCENE 2

DORANT: Everything that happens here – especially everything that's happening to me – is quite...unrealistic. I must see Lisette, and find out if she has had any joy trying to explain to her mistress and getting me out of this mess. If I could just catch her on her own –

Chase Number Three

(*The rules:*

– DORANT is looking for SILVIA but finds LISETTE.

– SILVIA is looking for her father – still rehearsing her text: 'If only you knew how much more all of this will make us love each other after we're married, if only you knew how grateful I'll be, how much I'll etc etc.'

– ARLECCHINO is looking for LISETTE.

– LISETTE is presumably going crazy.

– MR PROWDE sends MAURICE on to catch DORANT before he can get to SILVIA.)

MAURICE: Just a moment, Birmingham; could I have a brief word?

DORANT: What can I do for you, sir?

MAURICE: Have you been making suggestions to our Lisette?

DORANT: When one meets someone truly loveable it is hard not to talk like a lover.

MAURICE: And how does she take your speeches?

DORANT: Very lightly, sir.

MAURICE: You are amusing; are you...misleading her?

DORANT: No, I'm not; and if I were, would it concern you? Supposing that Lisette did have a penchant for me –

MAURICE: A 'penchant' for you – where did you pick that one up? Coming from a lad like you your vocabulary shows quite remarkable refinement.

DORANT: Sir, I shouldn't know how to talk any other way.

MAURICE: I imagine it is with just such flights of pretension that you have been assaulting our Lisette. Almost like a gentleman.

DORANT: I assure you, sir, I am not pretending to be anybody; but I am sure you didn't detain me simply in order to subject me to ridicule and that you do have something else you wanted to say to me? We were talking about Lisette: about my intentions towards her and why that should be any concern of yours –

MAURICE: Good heavens! I detect a certain touch of jealousy in the delivery of that line. Do calm down. Thank you. Now, you were telling me…supposing that Lisette had a penchant for you…and?

DORANT: And why should you be told if she did, sir.

MAURICE: Ah yes. That was it. Because…despite the musical comedy tone which I have heretofore affected, I should become quite melodramatic were she to love you; because – and I really don't want to discuss this – I forbid you any further intimate conversations with her; *not* because I'm afraid that she might actually fall for you, you understand – she seems to me to be above that sort of thing – but simply because I personally dislike having someone called Birmingham as a rival.

DORANT: I know just how you feel – because Birmingham, being your real, typical Birmingham sort, doesn't much like having you as his either.

MAURICE: He must be patient.

DORANT: Yes, he must. Do you love her a lot, sir?

MAURICE: Enough to make her a serious proposal once I have successfully concluded certain rather delicate negotiations. If you see what I mean.

DORANT: I rather think I do. In which case, of course, she must love you.

MAURICE: What do you think? Aren't I worth loving?

DORANT: You're not by any chance fishing for compliments from an acknowledged rival, are you?

MAURICE: A sensible riposte and one I shall forgive; but – and it's too mortifying really – I can't honestly say that she does love me – and I'm not telling you this because I have to, as I'm sure you are aware – I just happen to think one should be frank in this sort of situation.

DORANT: You amaze me, sir; Lisette is not aware of your plans for her?

MAURICE: Lisette is fully aware of all the good I could do her, and yet appears not to be...susceptible – however I have high hopes that she'll soon be...sensible, and be mine. Thank you, that will be all – please don't make a scene. The fact that she doesn't really want me despite all I've got to give her will have to be sufficient consolation for the fact that you've got to let me take her even though you don't really want to... I hardly think that uniform's going to tip the balance in your favour, and let's face it, you're hardly equipped for fighting – someone like me.

SCENE 3

(*Enter SILVIA.*)

MAURICE: Ah, Lisette, there you are.

SILVIA: And what can I do for you sir, oh you look a bit upset to me.

MAURICE: Oh it's nothing, I've just been having a word with Birmingham here.

SILVIA: He looks a bit upset too – have you been telling him off?

DORANT: The master has been telling me how much he loves you, Lisette.

SILVIA: Well that's not my fault is it?

DORANT: And telling me not to love you.

SILVIA: Well he'd better tell me not to be so attractive then, hadn't he?

MAURICE: I can't prevent him loving you, Lisette darling, but I do rather mind him saying it to you.

SILVIA: Oh he doesn't say it anymore: he just repeats it.

MAURICE: Well he will at least avoid repeating it while I'm in the room. You may go, Birmingham.

DORANT: I'm waiting for her to tell me to.

MAURICE: I'm sorry?

SILVIA: He said he's waiting; you'll have to wait, too.

DORANT: Do you like The Master?

SILVIA: Do I love him, you mean? Well let's just say I don't
think it's going to be worth anyone's while telling me not
to.

DORANT: You aren't playing with me?

MAURICE: You may go now. Apparently this isn't one of my
more convincing roles. Excuse me, but to whom am I
talking?

DORANT: You're talking to Birmingham.

MAURICE: Well would he mind leaving?

DORANT: This hurts.

SILVIA: Oh that's enough now or he's going to get angry.

DORANT: (*Aside to SILVIA.*) Perhaps you don't want anything
better.

MAURICE: That'll do, thank you.

DORANT: You never said anything about loving someone else,
Lisette.

(*Exit DORANT.*)

SCENE 4

SILVIA: I think not loving a man like that would smack rather
of ingratitude, don't you?

(*MAURICE laughs; music. Enter MR PROWDE.*)

PROWDE: And what have you got to laugh about, Maurice?

MAURICE: Dorant has just made a splendidly angry exit
because I (*CHORD.*) forced him (*CHORD.*) to leave (*CHORD.*)
Lisette.

SILVIA: What on earth had you been saying to him in your
little *tête-à-tête.*

MAURICE: I have never seen a grown man so intrigued or so
distressed.

PROWDE: I am not at all sorry to see the boy hoist with his
own petard – and after all it's not as if he's had too hard a
time of it up till now – you could hardly have been more
entertaining if you had tried, daughter – but now, I agree
– I think we've gone far enough.

MAURICE: But how far exactly have we gone, sister?

SILVIA: Oh! I rather think I'm going to be happy.

MAURICE: 'Oh!' – *feel* the sweet certainty with which that syllable *was* inflected.

PROWDE: Daughter, are you anticipating that the boy will go so far as to get down on his knees and propose while he still thinks you're the maid?

SILVIA: Yes, Father dear, I am anticipating.

MAURICE: I love it when you act. 'Father Dear.' Now we have given our Shrew I suppose we're going to be all sweetness and light.

SILVIA: You don't miss a word.

MAURICE: 'Ah-ha! Now I take my revenge!' You pulled me up so short over my turns of phrase: it seems only fair I should now have a little fun with yours. Rest assured you're quite as amusing ecstatic as you were anxious.

PROWDE: At least you've got me on your side; you go ahead and do whatever you see *fit*.

SILVIA: Oh if you knew how grateful I'll be. Dorant and I, we were made for one another. He'll have to marry me – if you only knew how much I'll be in his debt too, after everything he's going through for me – and how much I'll cherish the memory of all the ridiculous things he's said – and if you knew how much more all of this is going to make us love each other after we're married – he won't ever be able to remember how we met without loving me, and I won't be able to think about it without loving him. You've made us happy for life by letting me do this; our marriage won't be like other people's. It won't be like other people's. It won't be like other people's; it'll be an adventure, even talking about it makes me want to cry; and to think it all happened by chance! I'm so lucky. I am so happy. I am so…

MAURICE: …good at making long speeches. Funny how eloquent cheap emotions can be.

PROWDE: Of course we all find romantic fiction charming – especially when it comes true. Do you think you can actually make it happen?

SILVIA: It already has. He's quite overcome. I await my
captive.

MAURICE: The cage may be a little more gilded than the
bird expects, but I'm not sure he's at all happy with the
prospect of captivity, I find his plight rather moving.

SILVIA: The more it costs him to make up his mind the more
he's worth to me. He thinks he can only have me at the
expense of disobeying his father. He thinks he is betraying
both The Family and The Family Fortune. Hardly
inconsiderable obstacles. I shall delight in triumphing
over them. But I want to snatch my victory from the jaws
of opposition, not to have him hand it to me on a plate. I
want a battle royal between Reason and Passion.

MAURICE: And you want Reason to be lost.

PROWDE: What you actually want is for him to suffer the
full imaginary consequences of the step he will think he
is making. Strange how Self-Respect can lead one to a
monstrous disregard for others.

MAURICE: Oh women are like that: they understand that
Vanity and Self-Respect are the same thing.
(*A glorious scream from LISETTE; ARLECCHINO has finally not
been able to wait any longer.*)

SCENE 5

PROWDE: Ah, that must be Lisette. I wonder what she wants.
(*Enter LISETTE in violent déshabille. ARLECCHINO can be heard
warming up for his big scene.*)

LISETTE: Sir, you did say you were leaving him up to me, that
you were placing him entirely in my hands; well I have
taken you at your word. I've gone to work on him as if I
was on one of my own jobs and, as you are about to see, a
very good job has been done too. He's all nice and ready.
What d'you want me to do with him now? Is Madam going
to hand him over?

PROWDE: Well, daughter, speak now or for ever hold your
peace.

SILVIA: You can have him, Lisette; I hereby renounce any
prior claim I may have in the matter, and hereby swear

that I have no interest in any hearts except those I have, as you put it, got nice and ready all by myself.

LISETTE: You really want me to marry him. Sir really wants me to marry him too.

PROWDE: Yes; if he'll have you. What does he see in you?

MAURICE: I can see no just impediment –

LISETTE: Neither can I and thank you all very much –

(*LISETTE goes to exit and get to work, but:*)

PROWDE: Oh – just one minor proviso; so that we're not held responsible for any possible consequences – you'll have to give him just a hint as to who you really are.

LISETTE: If I give him a hint, he'll get it.

PROWDE: I'm sure he's nice and ready enough to be able to stand the shock. He doesn't seem the oversensitive type.

(*ARLECCHINO and his preparations for the scene cannot be ignored any longer.*)

LISETTE: That's him looking for me. Everybody off please; this is my big scene.

PROWDE: Quite. Shall we go?

SILVIA: Gladly.

MAURICE: Do let's.

(*They exit. LISETTE arranges herself and the lighting. She may possibly sneak MAURICE back on to provide romantic accompaniment; if so, she also dismisses him later.*)

SCENE 6

(*Enter ARLECCHINO.*)

ARLECCHINO: Darling, at last. Now that I've found you I'll never let you go – every moment away from you has been sheer hell – I was afraid perhaps you didn't want to see me again.

LISETTE: Yes, I must say, it was something like that.

ARLECCHINO: Darling, don't you know that I'd die? You don't want me to die, do you?

LISETTE: No I don't, darling, you have no idea how much you're worth to me –

ARLECCHINO: [Ah! Hearing you say that makes me feel so much better.]

LISETTE: And you mustn't ever doubt the depth of my feelings for you –

ARLECCHINO: [I would like to kiss every one of those words and pluck them from your lips with mine.]

LISETTE: But you were being so very pressing on the subject of our marriage, and my – father had not yet given me permission to give you my answer; however I have just spoken to him and he has told me that I can tell you that you can ask him for my hand any time you want.

ARLECCHINO: Just before I ask him for it – let me ask you for it – (*He produces a script which he has prepared earlier.*) 'I wish to tender unto it my heartfelt thanks for its graciousness in permitting itself to be joined in union with mine which is not in the same league at all.'

LISETTE: You may borrow my hand sir, on one condition; that you never return it.

ARLECCHINO: [Dear little chunky juicy hand-baby], I am lucky to get hold of it under any circumstances whatsoever. 'The honour you do me is great. The only problem here is the honour I'm doing you.'

LISETTE: You do me much more than I deserve.

ARLECCHINO: Ah. No. No. [No; *you* do *me* more than *I* deserve.]

LISETTE: To me your love is like a gift from Heaven.

ARLECCHINO: Oh it's nothing really.

LISETTE: But I really don't deserve it.

ARLECCHINO: Wait till you see it in the daylight.

LISETTE: You have no idea how embarrassing I find your modesty.

ARLECCHINO: You have no idea how modest I really am.

LISETTE: No, really, sir, must I spell it out, I am the one who is being honoured.

ARLECCHINO: [Ahi! I don't know where to put myself.]

LISETTE: Yes, believe me, sir, I know my place.

ARLECCHINO: I know mine, too. And the people I know there, they aren't up to much, and you won't be either. When you know. Them. But that's the funny thing about getting to know me, you never know what's at the bottom of the bag.

LISETTE: (*Aside.*) I always think there's something not quite right about men who apologise, don't you? What are you actually trying to say?

ARLECCHINO: The Cat's in the Bag. Waiting to be let out.

LISETTE: Yes. And. You've got me worried now. Are you trying to say that you're not –
(*ARLECCHINO lets the cat out of the bag.*)
I think we'd better have a little talk.

ARLECCHINO: *Aspetto!* (*In order to try and explain, he goes back to a earlier scene and sets it up again.*) Madam; do you remember: The first time I saw you our Love was born, the second time –

LISETTE: – the second time he started to grow up and now he's Big Boy, yes yes.

ARLECCHINO: Okay; now; is he Healthy? *Robusto?* How does he feel about working for a living? Does he like little rooms? Garages, for instance.

LISETTE: I don't think I can stand very much more of this. Who are you?

ARLECCHINO: *Io sono…*have you ever seen a fake five-pound note? A fake ten-pound note? *Io sono…* I am… I am a bit like a fake five-pound note –

LISETTE: Go on. What's your name.

ARLECCHINO: (*Aside.*) My name? If I say I'm Arlecchino, will she want to marry-me-no.

LISETTE: Well?

ARLECCHINO: [Madam, this isn't easy, alright?] Do you like gentlemen?

LISETTE: What sort of gentlemen?

ARLECCHINO: Gentlemen's gentlemen.

LISETTE: This isn't Mr Dorant I'm talking to is it?

ARLECCHINO: He's my guv'nor.

LISETTE: You bastard. You-mean-he – no!

ARLECCHINO: (*Aside.*) [Well at least it rhymed]

LISETTE: Ape!
(*LISETTE beats up ARLECCHINO.*)

ARLECCHINO: (*Apart.*) [Not bad the gymnastics, eh?]

LISETTE: And here's me spending the entire evening trying to impress *him* and wearing myself out feeling inferior to a showman's bleeding monkey.

ARLECCHINO: I'm sorry. But if being Loved is as good as being Posh, I can do it just as well as he does.

LISETTE: You've got to laugh really haven't you, him and his Posh, 'cause if you didn't laugh – never mind, eh? I'm sure I'm Posh enough to handle the situation. At least I'm sure I'm quite Posh enough for you.

ARLECCHINO: [Really?]

LISETTE: Really. So what if I've been made a fool – (*She takes his hand as if to make up.*) – A Gentleman's Gentleman deserves a Lady's Maid.

ARLECCHINO: A Lady's Maid?

LISETTE: She's my guv'nor. Or whatever you say when it's a woman who's the guv'nor.

ARLECCHINO: [Minx!]

LISETTE: Go on, feel free.

ARLECCHINO: And there's me spending the entire evening going all ashamed of my having no money.

LISETTE: Now let's talk business. D'you love me?

ARLECCHINO: [God!] *Si. Oui.* Yes. What I call you has changed but what I see has not changed. Anyway –

LISETTE: – anyway we did swear to love one another for ever disregarding any minor violations of the agreed rules of socially acceptable behaviour which we might find ourselves inspired to commit. So, not too much harm done is there – pretend nothing's happened. I don't want anyone laughing at us. (*Checks through the keyhole to see that no one has seen anything.*) It's your guv'nor – he's coming in here – (*Enter DORANT.*) Looks to me like he still hasn't worked out what's going on with my mistress; don't tell him anything – we'll leave things just the way they are – I am, sir, your humble servant.

ARLECCHINO: Madam; I'm one too.

(*Exit LISETTE.*)

SCENE 7

DORANT: Have you told her who you are yet?

ARLECCHINO: [Oh God yes. Poor child!] I said to her, '[I am called] Arlecchino, I am the Chauffeur'; 'Oh really dear boy,' she said, 'everyone has to have a name, everyone has to have a uniform. So, yours is not a suit – well, it suits you.'

DORANT: This is another one of your ridiculous stories.

ARLECCHINO: So I'm going to marry her.

DORANT: What! You proposed? She's accepted?

ARLECCHINO: [Oh yes of course she'd have to be mentally ill to do that.]

DORANT: You're making this up; she doesn't know who you are.

ARLECCHINO: You want to make a bet I marry her with my boots on? You make me angry – with my overalls on, okay? I would like you to know that when I love somebody it does not break easy, and that I don't need your suit for me to do it, and I have my clothes back now thank you.

DORANT: You're having me on – it's inconceivable…and I can see it's high time I had a word with Mr Prowde.

ARLECCHINO: [Who?] Oh, Farther in Lore. Splendid Old Chap. Got him right on board. Lovely Old Boy. Absolutely your first-class old boy. You were saying?

DORANT: You're incredible, you know that? Have you seen Lisette?

ARLECCHINO: Lisette? No. Possible she did pass before my eyes, but a real gentleman doesn't really notice – the Maid. I leave that sort of thing up to you.

DORANT: And you're insane. Now get out.

ARLECCHINO: Your manners leave a little to he desired my boy. But you'll find that comes with experience. (*Exit ARLECCHINO. Enter ARLECCHINO.*) When I am married, [we will he equal], you and me.
(*Enter SILVIA.*)

[Oh, here is your maid.] Good Evening Lisette. May I
recommend the Birmingham. The boy's not without his
redeeming features.
(*Exit ARLECCHINO.*)

SCENE 8

DORANT: Well you can understand why people love her…
Damn Maurice for getting there first.

SILVIA: Where have you been, sir? Ever since that scene with
Master Maurice I've been hunting for you all over the
place to tell you what I've been telling Mr Prowde.

DORANT: How odd. I haven't been hiding myself. And what
have you been telling him?

SILVIA: Well I can understand him being so cold, he – I told
him, straight out I told him what I thought about this
chauffeur and I said clearly the man's got no conscience
and isn't at all suitable, I pointed out in no uncertain terms
the very least he can do is postpone the wedding but no
he wasn't having any of it. And just between you and me
there's talk of it being time to book the church, so you'll
have to give the game up now, won't you?

DORANT: I intend to. I'll leave a note explaining the situation
to Mr Prowde and then slip off incognito.

SILVIA: Slip off. That wasn't the idea at all.

DORANT: I think that would be best, don't you?

SILVIA: But – not particularly.

DORANT: I can't think what else to do in this situation, except
actually tell him myself of course, and I can't see me doing
that. Besides, there are other reasons why I must leave; I
really can't go on with this any longer.

SILVIA: Since I've no idea what these reasons of yours are I
can't really sympathise and I can't really try and talk you
out of them, can I? – and it's hardly my place to ask you to
tell me what they are.

DORANT: It should be quite easy for you to suspect what they
are, Lisette.

SILVIA: Well it had occurred to me that possibly you had taken
a dislike to the master's daughter.

DORANT: Is that all that has occurred to you?

SILVIA: Well of course there are certain other things I might imagine – but then, I'm no fool, and I'm not vain enough to dwell on things like that.

DORANT: And not brave enough to talk about them – still, I don't expect anything you'd have to say would be anything I'd want to hear. Goodbye, Lisette.

SILVIA: I can see I'm going to have to spell it out, you really don't understand do you?

DORANT: Oh but I do. Perfectly. And making things clearer wouldn't make them any easier, so please, remain incomprehensible until after I've gone.

SILVIA: You're not actually going to go are you?

DORANT: You seem very afraid that I might change my mind.

SILVIA: How very sweet of you to be so perceptive.

DORANT: How very frank of you to say so.

(DORANT makes his exit. During his exit:)

SILVIA: If he leaves the room, how can I love him, I shan't hove him, I shan't ever marry him... Oh look he's stopping. He's thinking about it, he's looking to see if I'm turning my head – and I – and I don't know what to do to make him come back, I... Wouldn't it be funny if he did go, after I've gone to all this trouble. Well I suppose that's it then. He's gone. I don't have as much hold over him as I thought. God that brother of mine's useless, he went about it completely the wrong way. People who don't care about anything always ruin everything. And I was doing so well. Not much of an ending is it? Perhaps he'll come back on. I really do think he's coming back now – *(But he isn't.)*
(She goes to exit; at which moment of course DORANT comes back on.)

– I take it all back of course I love him – I'll pretend to leave – he'll have to stop me – it's always best when the reconciliation is a bit more difficult for the man –

DORANT: Stay – please – there's something I have to say to you.

SILVIA: To me, sir?

DORANT: I'm finding it very hard to leave without having
made you see that it's not my fault.

SILVIA: Oh, sir, you don't have to explain yourself to me. It's
not hard at all; I'm only the maid, as you've made me only
too well aware.

DORANT: I have? And who do you see having to put up with
everything and not saying a word – me – I don't see you've
any reason to find your position in all this particularly
difficult.

SILVIA: There's a really good answer to that. It's just that I
can't bring myself to say it.

DORANT: No, please, let's have it, I'd like nothing better
than to be told I've got this all wrong. Oh, but what am I
saying? Maurice loves you.

SILVIA: That's right.

DORANT: And you're quite happy that he loves you – as one
can see from the extreme vigour with which you sought
to prevent me from leaving – in which case of course you
couldn't possibly love me.

SILVIA: I'm happy. Who told you that? And I couldn't possibly
love you. How would you know? You're very sure about
everything.

DORANT: Listen, Lisette, for God's sake, please, tell me what's
going on. Please.

SILVIA: What can you tell a man when he's leaving you?

DORANT: I won't leave, ever.

SILVIA: OH STOP IT. Listen, if you love me, stop asking me
all these questions. You're scared I might have nothing to
say – and then you love it when I don't say anything – and
anyway what have my feelings got to do with you?

DORANT: What have they got to do with me? Lisette, you
can't still seriously doubt that I'm mad about you.

SILVIA: No I can't. You say it to me so very often that I'm
obliged to believe it, so why must you keep on trying to
persuade me of the fact and what do you want me to do
about it. Sir. Now I am going to be frank with you. You
love me; but your falling in love really isn't anything very
serious. Should you ever want to fall out of it again you'll

find Life makes that relatively easy for the likes of you. The
distance between you and me; all the attractive women
you're going to meet; how keen they're going to be on
your being keen on them, all the distractions available to a
young gent like you…all that'll get you out of what you're
trying so hard to talk me into. I expect that when you leave
here you'll have a good laugh about it all – and that'll be
alright for you. But I, Sir, if I ever look back, as I'm rather
afraid I shall, if I let myself succumb, what am I going to
have to protect me against what you will have done to
me? Who's going to compensate me if you've ruined me?
Who's my heart going to get in as a replacement? You do
realise that if I love you then all the things that matter most
to me aren't going to matter any more. So you just stop for
a bit and think about the state I'll be in. And be kind to
me, sir. Conceal your love. And as for me – well, I should
think twice about telling you I loved you in the state you're
in – if I were to reveal my feelings that might really drive
you mad, and anyway, as you can see, I'm concealing
them from you.

DORANT: Oh darling Lisette. The way you talk, the things
you say – go right through me. I adore you. I respect you.
And what class I am, what Family I'm from, how much
Money I have or won't have – well you make all that seem
inconsequential. I'd be a fool to let my Pride hold out
against you any longer. I offer you my hand, and believe
me, my heart's in it.

SILVIA: Oh of course I couldn't really refuse an offer from
a gent like you could I? And I can hardly conceal how
happy I am to have been made it, can I? And do you really
think this will last?

DORANT: You do love me?

SILVIA: No. No. And if you ask me just one more time that will
be it.

DORANT: You can't scare me away.

SILVIA: What about Maurice? Aren't you bothered about him?

DORANT: No Lisette, Maurice doesn't bother me; you don't
love him; you can't fool me any more. You care. You care

about me. I know you do, otherwise I wouldn't be feeling what I am feeling, and nothing you can say can take that away from me.

SILVIA: Oh I shan't try to, you can keep your feeling. And now what are you going to do?

(*DORANT kneels.*)

DORANT: Be mine.

SILVIA: Oh so you're going to marry me, and never mind Society and never mind your Father and never mind the Money.

DORANT: My father will understand as soon as he sees you; I'm sure my money will be enough for the two of us, and who you are matters more than what society you keep, so please don't argue with me any more, because I won't ever change my mind.

SILVIA: He won't ever change. Do you have any idea how charming I find you, Dorant?

DORANT: Don't lock your heart up any longer. Let it say what it wants to say.

SILVIA: Alright then. This is finally it. You – you won't ever change.

DORANT: No. No Lisette, I won't.

SILVIA: This is Love.

(*The rest of THE COMPANY enter, in evening dress, applauding, with champagne.*)

SCENE 9

SILVIA: Ah, Father. You always said I should belong to Mr Dorant. Well do come in, come in and watch your daughter obey you with the very greatest of pleasure.

DORANT: What is this? You're her father?

SILVIA: Yes. You see we both had the same idea of getting to know each other. And after that – well, what else can I tell you? – you obviously love me, there was never really any doubt about that – and if you are in any doubt about my feelings – well I think you can judge how I feel about you from the great lengths I have gone to get you where I wanted you.

PROWDE: Do you recognise this letter? That was how I knew about your disguise – though she only knew because you told her.

DORANT: I can't tell you how happy I am. But I will just say that what makes me happiest is having had the chance to prove myself.

MAURICE: I trust Dorant will forgive me for making life so difficult for Birmingham?

DORANT: No he won't forgive you for it. He thanks you for it.
(*SILVIA takes off her apron.*)

EPILOGUE WITH MUSIC

(*The SERVANTS clear up now the MASTERS and MISTRESSES have finished their game. The house is dark and quiet, except for the piano.*)

ARLECCHINO: [Cheer up, missus.] You didn't get the money – you still got me.

LISETTE: Oh thanks a lot. That's very nice – for you.

ARLECCHINO: [That's true.] Before we found out who we really were you had lots of money and no class. Now you got no money. But you got plenty of class. You fancy a dance then?
(*The End.*)

CPSIA information can be obtained
at www.ICGtesting.com
Printed in the USA
LVHW011812091222
734912LV00003B/767

9 780948 230585